CW00713022

Quick Japanese

Diethard Lübke
Regina Lübke

TEACH YOURSELF BOOKS
Hodder and Stoughton

British Library Cataloguing in Publication Data

ISBN 0 340 52935 0

First published 1987 by Langenscheidt Publishers

© 1990 Hodder and Stoughton Ltd

Typeset by Graphicraft Typesetters Ltd, Hong Kong.
Printed in Great Britain for the educational publishing division of Hodder and Stoughton Ltd, Mill Road, Dunton Green, Sevenoaks, Kent by Richard Clay Ltd, Bungay.

Contents

Introduction

You probably know how it feels: you arrive in a foreign country and don't understand the language. This makes you unsure of yourself and detracts from the enjoyment of the trip. You don't understand the signs at the airport, the station or by the roadside. Hotel staff, taxi drivers and sales assistants speak little or no English. You don't feel up to ordering in local restaurants and end up eating at the hotel most of the time. Everywhere you go, you are dependent on a guide, and you feel helpless and illiterate in a highly civilised country.

Quick & Easy Japanese is a course of self study that aims to help you understand and speak simple Japanese, the sort of Japanese you will need on a visit to Japan. It cannot promise that at the end you will be speaking perfectly, but by enabling you to learn the most important words and expressions a visitor needs, it will undoubtedly help to improve your experience of Japan and get more out of your time abroad.

The course does not require a great deal of study or concentration, but it does offer more than a phrasebook and you will find that if you are prepared to spend a certain amount of time, even at odd hours of the day, in going through each unit in turn and testing your knowledge carefully, you will begin to acquire a basic knowledge of the language.

The course consists of 20 units, each dealing with a particular aspect of a visit to Japan. Within each unit are groups of words and phrases relevant to the topic. All words and idioms are written in Japanese script, followed by an English transcription and finally a translation into English. It is essential to give Japanese characters, as this will enable you to read simple signs, timetables, etc. It also means that you will be able to show the book to a Japanese person if you get into difficulties.

The exercises which follow are of two types: those which require a test of memory to see if you can ask a question or say a phrase which was given on the previous page, and those which ask you to adapt a phrase to suit your own purposes.

At the end of each unit is a short information section which you will find useful on your visit, and the book ends with a an English–Japanese vocabulary list containing all the words used in the book.

Ideally, you should begin the course at least six weeks before setting out on your trip. Take the book with you so that you can practise the words and phrases you have learnt. The Japanese generally assume that foreign visitors will not speak their language, so they are not only surprised but will be twice as friendly and helpful when they hear a visitor making an effort to speak Japanese. Don't be afraid to try – you are bound to make mistakes, but the most important thing is that you will have made yourself understood.

How to Speak Japanese

Contrary to popular opinion, Japanese is not a difficult language to speak. In fact, apart from the writing systems, Japanese is simple to learn in comparison with European languages. Words are short and easy to remember, and many of them are taken from English, though of course they are pronounced in a Japanese fashion. Examples:

bēkon (bacon), kamera (camera), fōku (fork), gaido (guide), hoteru (hotel), orenji (orange), serufu sābisu (self-service).

Pronunciation

The pronunciation and intonation of Japanese should not be a problem for English speakers. The five short vowels – **a, e, i, o, u** – are pronounced in a similar way to English, but spoken more briskly. The vowels **i, o** and **u** are often almost inaudible, particularly when **i** follows **ch, h** or **sh**, and when **u** follows **f, k, s** or **ts**. Vowels written with a line above are long and should be pronounced at approximately double their normal length.

Consonants are much as in English except for **f** (pronounced rather like **h**) and **r** (rather like **l**, which does not exist in Japanese). Note that **g** is always hard. Japanese also has long consonants, which are pronounced like double letters.

Stress is not generally carried by any particular syllable in a word.

Japan Travel-Phone is a newly installed, free telephone service. An English-speaking travel expert helps you to solve language problems and gives you travel information. Dial 502-1461 in Tokyo, and 371-5649 in Kyoto. If you phone from outside Tokyo and Kyoto, dial 106 and say in English: 'Collect call, TiAiCi please.' You will at once be put through to the Tourist Information Centre.

Japanese Writing Systems

Japanese writing consists of 3 systems:

Kanji = symbols for **words**; they were introduced from China in the 4th century.

Hiragana, Katakana = two symbol systems for **syllables**; they have been used since the 8th century.

Hiragana is used for suffixes, prefixes and words other than nouns, verbs and adjectives (unless there is no Kanji word). Katakana is used for foreign words and names, and words you want to stress.

Kanji

Introductory remark: You already know that words are not always written in letters, but that a symbol can represent a word or phrase:

$ dollar	& and	§ section	1 one
£ pound	= equals	⊗ to eat	2 two
% per cent	© copyright	Ⓐ Mercedes-Benz	3 three

Three are more than 50,000 Japanese word symbols, but only about 5,000 are used. An educated Japanese knows about 3,000 word symbols; after having attended school for 6 years, a Japanese child should know at least 1,000.

Japanese Writing Systems

The word symbols consist of up to 23 strokes, the sequence of which is precisely stipulated when writing:

(kan) = standard; mirror

Not all word symbols are as difficult as this one. You will be able to remember the following ones easily:

山 (yama)	three peaks =	mountain
田 (ta)	ground with furrows =	field
木 (ki)	trunk with branches =	tree
森 (mori)	many trees =	forest
口 (kuchi)	opening =	mouth, gate
雨 (u)	drops =	rain
中 (naka)	stroke through the middle =	centre
上 (ue)	upward stroke =	up
下 (shita)	downward stroke =	down

Complicated word symbols can be taken apart in order to give clues to understanding:

問 = question
From 門 *a gate* and 口 *a mouth*. Questions come from the gate of the mouth.

安 = peaceful
女 *a woman* in 宀 *a house* is peaceful

母 = mother
Combination of 女 *a woman* and the two *dots*, representing a woman nursing.

Hiragana and Katakana

For better understanding, both writing systems are arranged according to the Latin alphabet (first: Hiragana, second: Katakana):

Japanese Writing Systems

	a	e	i	o	u	—	
—	あア a	えエ e	いイ i	おオ o	うウ u	—	
h	はハ ha(wa)	へへ he(e)	ひヒ hi	ほホ ho	ふフ fu/hu	—	**h**
b	ばバ ba	べべ be	びビ bi	ぼボ bo	ぶブ bu	—	**b**
p	ぱパ pa	ぺぺ pe	ぴピ pi	ぽポ po	ぷプ pu	—	**p**
k	かカ ka	けケ ke	きキ ki	こコ ko	くク ku	—	**k**
g	がガ ga	げゲ ge	ぎギ gi	ごゴ go	ぐグ gu	—	**g**
m	まマ ma	めメ me	みミ mi	もモ mo	むム mu	—	**m**
n	なナ na	ねネ ne	にニ ni	のノ no	ぬヌ nu	んン n	**n**
r	らラ ra	れレ re	りリ ri	ろロ ro	るル ru	—	**r**
s	さサ sa	せセ se	しシ shi/si	そソ so	すス su	—	**s**
z	ざザ za	ぜゼ ze	じジ ji/zi	ぞゾ zo	ずズ zu	—	**z**
t	たタ ta	てテ te	ちチ chi/ti	とト to	つツ tsu/tu	—	**t**
d	だダ da	でデ de	ぢヂ ji/zi	どド do	づヅ zu	—	**d**
w	わワ wa	—	—	をヲ o	—	—	**w**
y	やヤ ya	—	—	よヨ yo	ゆユ yu	—	**y**
	a	e	i	o	u	—	

Introduction to Japanese Grammar

Nouns

1 There are no words for 'the' and 'a' in Japanese, and no separate genders.
2 Nouns do not have a plural form, so *shinbun* can mean 'one newspaper' or 'many newspapers'.
3 Japanese has a system of suffixes and prefixes which indicate what part the word plays in a sentence:

は	-wa	attached to the end of a word show that it is the subject
が	-ga	
を	-o	after a word shows that it is the direct object
に	-ni	indicates the indirect object
の	-no	is used to show possession (the genitive)

お **o-** and ご **go-** are added to the beginning of a word if you want to be particularly polite or formal, e.g.

お勘定を下さい。 The bill, please.
o-kanjo-o kudasái.　(= *Polite prefix* bill *direct object* please.)

Pronouns

Japanese uses very few pronouns and there are no relative pronouns. However, note that the suffix たち **-tachi** is added to form the plural:

私	watashi	I
私たち	watashi-tachi	we

Verbs

1 です　　desu　　to be / am / are / is
Japanese verbs have no person: **desu** is the verb 'to be', but it can also mean 'am, is, are' as well as 'he/she is, it is, we are, you are, they are'. There is no fixed word order in a sentence, but **desu** generally comes at the end.

Introduction to Japanese Grammar

2 Infinitive and present tense endings are:

う	-u ⎫	
る	-ru ⎭	
ます	-masu	is a polite present tense ending
ません	-masen	makes the verb negative

Examples:

あります	ari-masu	there is / there are
ありません	ari-masen	there is not / there are not

3 か **ka** at the end of a sentence is used to form a question:

英語の新聞がありますか。   Do you have an English paper?
eigo-no shimbun-ga   (= English-*genitive* paper-
  arimasu ka.   *subject* there is *interrogative*.)

4 When making a polite request, the ending て **-te** is added to the verb + **kudasái** (please / please give me):

行って下さい。   Let's go, please / Please go to...
it-te kudasái.

5 The suffix たい **-tai** is used when you want to say 'I / you would like to...', e.g.

したい。 shi-tai. I would like to do it.

Adjectives

Adjectives in Japanese end in the suffix い **-i**:

痛い	ita-i	painful
高い	taka-i	expensive, high

1 Greetings **2** How are you? **3** Mr, Mrs
4 I'm, there is **5** Understanding

1.1	はい	hai	yes, well, O.K.
	いいえ	iie	no
	こんにちは	konnichi-wa	hello! (*only during the day*)
	おはようございます	ohayō gozaimasu	Good morning!
	さようなら	sayōnara	Goodbye!
	すみません	sumimasen	Excuse me...
	下さい	kudasái	Please
	ありがとう	arigatō	Thank you!
	どうもありがとう	dōmo arigatō	Thank you very much!

1.2	はじめまして。	hagimemashite	How do you do?
	お元気ですか。	ogenki desu ka	How are you?
	元気です。	genki desu / arigato	Fine, thanks.
	ありがとう。		

1.3	さん	-san	Mr, Mrs, Miss (*suffix*)
	私	watashi	I
	あなた	anata	you
	私たち	watashi-tachi	**we**
	私の	watashi-no	my (= I-*genitive*)

田中さん	Mr / Mrs / Miss Tanaka
Tanaka-san.	

1 General Expressions

1.4

この	kono	this
と/そして	to / soshite	and
です	desu	to be / am / are / is
あります	ari-masu	there is / there are
ありません	ari-masen	there is not / there are not
どこですか。	doko desu ka	where is ...?
なんですか。	nan desu ka	what is it?

（私は）イギリス人です。
(Watashiwa) Igirisu-jin
   desu.
	I'm British.
	(= I-*subject* Britain-
	  person be.)

（あなたは）イギリス人ですか。
(Anatawa) Igirisu-jin
   desu ka.
	Are you British?
	(= Britain-person be
	  interrogative.)

1.5

わかりません。	wakarimasen.	I don't understand.
書いて下さい。	kaite kudasái.	Please write it down.
もういちど言ってください。	mō ichido itte kudasai.	Please repeat it.

General Expressions 1

1. It is morning. You say 'hello' to your Japanese friends:

   . . . .

2. You meet your Japanese friends during the day and you say 'hello' to them:

   . . . .

3. A Japanese asks you if you're British:

   . . . .

4. If you're British, you answer: . . . .

5. If you're not British, you answer: . . . .

6. You meet a Japanese, who gives you his calling card. You say 'Thank you' in Japanese:

   . . . .

7. You say 'goodbye' to him: . . . .

8. You have dialled the wrong telephone number. You say 'Excuse me' in Japanese:

   . . . .

1 General Expressions

- The Japanese avoid saying '**no**' because it would disturb 'social harmony'.

- If you know a person's name you should use his or her **last name** with the suffix -san instead of saying 'you'.

- When greeting, the Japanese **bow**, putting their hands on their thighs. The person with the higher social status is the first to rise. Shaking hands is rare and only practised between men.

- If you are invited to a Japanese person's home, you should **present** your host with something to eat or to drink (e.g. a bottle of whisky or a box of chocolates) instead of flowers. It is important for the present to be nicely wrapped, though it is never unwrapped in your presence.

- In 10 cities you have the possibility to visit Japanese **families** in their homes. Consult the following:

● Offices for Application

- *SAPPORO*
Sapporo Tourist Association
(0 11) 211-3341
- *TOKYO*
J.N.T.O. Tourist Information Centre
(03) 502-1461
- *YOKOHAMA*
Yokohama Municipal Tourist Association
(045) 641-5824
Kanagawa Prefectural Tourist Association
(045) 681-0007
- *NAGOYA*
Tourist & Foreign Trade Section
Nagoya City Office
(052) 961-1111
- *OTSU*

Tourist Section Otsu City Office
(0775) 23-1234
Otsu City Information Office
(0775) 22-3830
- *KYOTO*
Tourist Section
Kyoto City Government
(075) 752-0215
- *OSAKA*
Osaka Tourist Association
(06) 261-3948
Osaka Tourist Information Office
(06) 345-2189
- *KOBE*
Kobe International Tourist Association
(078) 232-1010

- *KURASHIKI*
Kurashiki Association for International Friendship
(0864) 22-5141
- *KAGOSHIMA*
Tourist Section
Kagoshima City Office
(0992) 24-1111
- *HIROSHIMA*
Hiroshima Tourist Association
(082) 247-6738
- *NARITA*
Narita City Tourist Information Office
(0476) 24-3198
J.N.T.O. New Tokyo Int'l Airport Office
(Narita)
(0476) 32-8711

- **Always be on time!**

- The Japanese expect everybody to be **properly dressed**. Even in the hot summer months, most Japanese men wear a white shirt with a tie and a dark pair of trousers

1 Customs **2** Documents **3** Nationality

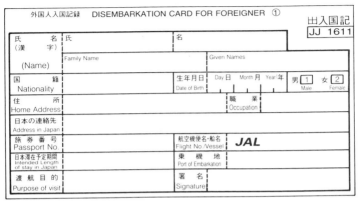

外国人入国記録 DISEMBARKATION CARD FOR FOREIGNER ① 出入国記 JJ 1611

氏　　　名 （漢　字） (Name)	氏 Family Name		名 Given Names	
国　　　籍 Nationality		生年月日 Date of Birth	Day日　Month月　Year年	男 1　女 2 Male　Female
住　　　所 Home Address			職　　業 Occupation	
日本の連絡先 Address in Japan				
旅　券　番　号 Passport No.		航空機便名・船名 Flight No./Vessel	***JAL***	
日本滞在予定期間 Intended Length of stay in Japan		乗　機　地 Port of Embarkation		
渡　航　目　的 Purpose of visit		署　名 Signature		

2.1	検査	kensa	control, check
	旅券検査	ryoken kensa	passport control
	居住者	kyojūsha	residents (*people living in Japan*)
	非居住者	hi kyojūsha	non-residents (*visitors, tourists*)
	荷物引取り	nimotsu hikitori	Baggage claim
	荷物	nimotsu	luggage (= cargo-thing)
	手荷物	tenimotsu	hand luggage
	鞄	kában	bag, briefcase
	税関	zeikan	customs (= entering-tax)

> 申告するものはありません。
> shinkoku suru mono-wa arimasen.
> 鞄を開けて下さい。
> kában-o akete kudasái.

> I've nothing to declare.
> (= Declare make thing-*subject* there is not.)
> Open your bag, please.
> (= Bag-*direct-object* open, please.)

2.2	旅券 パスポート	ryoken pasupōto	}	passport (= travelling-certificate)
	外人	gai-jin		foreigners (= outside-person)
	お名前	o-namae		name

2 Entering Japan

人名	jin-mei	first name
名刺	mei-shi	calling card
住所	jūsho	address

私はピーターと申します。 Watashi-wa Pītā to mōshimasu.	My name is Peter. (= I-*subject* Peter so be-called.)

2.3

国	kuni	nation
国籍	kokuseki	nationality
日本	Nihon	Japan (= sun-origin)
日本人	Nihon-jin	Japanese (= Japan-person)
英国／イギリス	Eikoku/Igirisu	Great Britain
英国人／ イギリス人	Eikoku jin/ Igirisu-jin	British
大使館	taishi-kan	embassy (= big-messenger-building)
領事館	ryōji-kan	consulate

（私は）イギリス人です。 (Watashi wa) Igirisu-jin desu	I'm British.
英国（イギリス）大使館 Eikoku (*or* Igirisu) taishikan	British Embassy
これを訳して下さい。 kore-o yaku shite kudasái.	Translate the following, please. (= This-*direct-object* translate make please.)
英語の新聞がありますか。 eigo-no shimbun-ga arimasu ka.	Do you have an English paper? (= English-*genitive* paper-subject there is *interrogative*.)
はいあります。 hai, arimasu.	Yes, I have. (= Yes, there is.)

You arrive in Tokyo by plane.

1. You are a foreigner. Where do you line up for passport control?

. . . .

2. Where do you pick up your luggage?

. . . .

3. Which sign indicates customs control?

. . . .

4. What are these called in Japanese?

. . . .

5. Your English-speaking guide gives you this card:

YOKO SAKAKIBARA

LICENSED GUIDE

**C/O MORITA, 2–10–10 IGUSA
SUGINAMI-KU, TOKYO 167
PHONE (03) 396–7426**

What do you call this card in Japanese ? . . . .

6. You would like to ring the British Embassy. 'British Embassy' in Japanese is:

. . . .

2 Entering Japan

What do these symbols/characters stand for in Japanese and what is their English translation?

7. 日本　Jap.: . . . . 　Engl.: . . . .
   (sun-origin)

8. 人　Jap.: . . . . 　Engl.: . . . .
   (side view of a man)

9. 外人　Jap.: . . . . 　Engl.: . . . .

10. How do you think these characters could be translated into English?

    外国　Engl.: . . . .

- **Embassy** in Tokyo: **British** 1 Ichibancho Chiyoda-ku.

- Goods that can be brought into Japan **tax-free**:
  14 ounces of tobacco, or 400 cigarettes, or 100 cigars; 3 bottles of alcohol; 75 ml of perfume; 2 watches and other personal valuables up to a value of 100,000 yen.

- Plants, fruits, and vegetables must not be brought into the country.

- Instead of a signature the Japanese use a **personal seal** (hanko はんこ). Documents are sealed, because signatures are not legally binding.

- If you would like to contact a Japanese privately or for business reasons, it is necessary to have a **calling card**. One side should be printed in English, the other in Japanese: Give your name, title and profession. Calling cards are always carefully studied in order to find out the social position of the owner.

- The Japanese have a strong sense of **national pride**. Less than 1% of the population is of non-Japanese origin.

---

1 Car **2** Roads **3** Petrol **4** Taxi

ミツビシ

MITSUBISHI INTERNATIONAL

トヨタ **TOYOTA**

 ニツサン

ホンダ

マツダ

3.1	車	kuruma	car
	運転する	unten-suru	to drive
	運転手	unten-shu	driver (= drive-hand)
	運転免許証	unten-menkyoshō	driving licence
	レンタカー	renta-kā	car rental
3.2	道路	dōro	street, avenue
	…道り	dōri	. . . street (*with the name of the street*)
	国道	kokudō	road
	高速道路	kōsoku-dōro	motorway (= high-speed-road)
	料金所	ryōkinsho	toll gate
	出口	deguchi	exit
	橋	hashi	bridge
	駐車禁止	chūsha kinshi.	No parking.

3 Car and Taxi

3.3

ガソリンスタンド	gasorin-sutando	petrol station
ガソリン	gasorin	petrol
オイル	oiru	oil

満タンにして下さい。 mantan-ni shite kudasái	Fill it up, please. (= Fill-up-*indirect-object* make please.)

3.4

タクシー	takushī	taxi
空車	kūsha	for hire, free

ここへ行って下さい。 Koko-e itte kudasái.	Take me to this place, please.* (= There-to drive please.)
…ホテルへ行って下さい。 . . . hoteru-e itte kudasái.	Please take me to the . . . Hotel. (= . . .-Hotel-to drive, please.)
いくらですか。 ikura desu ka?	How much is it? (= How-much be *interrogative*.)

1. How do you say 'car' in Japanese?

. . . .

*You show the driver the address and the map of the area.

2. Where is the car in the illustration standing?

. . . .

3. You want the attendant to fill it up.
   You say to him:

. . . .

4. What is this car called? . . . .

5. What sign behind the windscreen shows you that the taxi is

   free? . . . .

6. You would like to go to the Nippon Hotel.
   You say to the driver:

. . . .

7. You ask the driver how much you owe him:

. . . .

Say in Japanese what these traffic signs indicate.

8. . . . .   9. . . . .   10. . . . .

3 Car and Taxi

- In Japan you drive on the left-hand side of the road. The amount of **traffic** is enormous and traffic jams are frequent. Travel by car is usually slow. There is a speed limit of 80 or 100 km/h (50 mph) on major roads and 40 km/h (25 mph) on other roads.

- A large number of **traffic signs** are written in Japanese, which you must understand if you are planning to drive in Japan.

- The international **driving licence** is not valid in Japan. A Japanese driving licence can be applied for at the following address: Samezu, 1-15-5 Higashi-oi, Sinagawaku, Tokyo, Tel. 474-1174.

- All dual carriageways are **toll roads**.

- **Drinking and driving** is strictly prohibited.

- **Cyclists** are allowed to ride on the pavement.

- You can recognize a **taxi** by a characteristic advertisement symbol on the middle of the roof, which at night is illuminated.

- Most **taxi drivers do not speak English**. Before taking a taxi, ask someone to write down the address in Japanese, with a sketch if possible to show the taxi driver. He may have to ask a passer-by for further information.

- For reasons of safety, the passenger cannot open the right-hand door of the taxi. The left-hand door to the sidewalk can only be opened by the driver.

1 In town **2** Directions

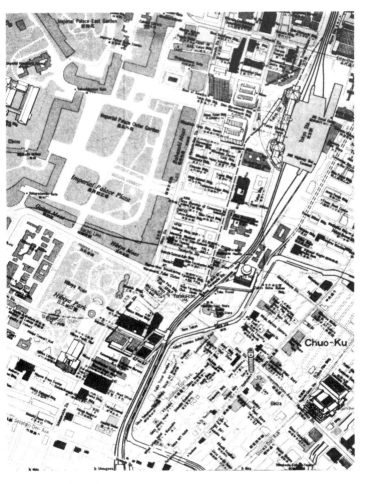

東京 Tokyo（市内）

4 Finding your Way

4.1

図	zu	drawing
地図	chi-zu	map (= earth-map)
道路地図	dōro-chizu	road map
市	shi	town
市内	shi-nai	city centre
市内地図	shinai-chizu	city map
区	ku	municipal district
丁目	chōme	block

市内地図を一枚下さい。	A map, please.
shinai-chizu-o ichimai kudasái.	(= Map-*direct-object* one piece please.)

4.2

どこ	doko	where
あそこ	asóko	there
左	hidári	left
右	migi	right
まっすぐ	massúgu	straight ahead
北	kita	north
南	minami	south
東	higashi	east
西	nishi	west

駅はどこですか。	Where is the station?
eki-wa doko desu ka?	(= Station-*subject* where be *interrogative*.)
東口 higashi-guchi	East Entrance / Exit
西出口 nishi-deguchi	West Exit
左へ hidári-e	To the left.
右へ migi-e	To the right.

You are in a Japanese city.

1. You would like to buy a city map.
   You say to the salesperson:

. . . .

2. You cannot find the station.
   You ask a policeman:

   . . . .

You have arrived by train at a large station.

3. You're looking for the 'west exit'
   You ask the stationmaster:

   . . . .

4. He points you in the right direction, saying:

   . . . .

5. You say 'Thank you': . . . .

Which may must the cars turn?

6. . . . .   7. . . . .

8. . . . .

4 Finding your Way

FOR TAXI DRIVER　ご案内図
大阪東急ホテル　TEL 373-2411
〒530 大阪市北区茶屋町7番20号

至新大阪
TO SHINOSAKA

至京都
TO KYOTO

大阪東急ホテル
OSAKA
TOKYU HOTEL

CHAYA MACHI

YANMER
DIESEL

大阪鉄道管理局

HANKYU
UMEDA
STATION

UMEDA
KOMA

TO NAKANOSHIMA

状大阪駅
OSAKA STATION

N

HANKYU
DEPARTMENT
STORE

TO KOBE

大阪市北区茶屋町7番20号　TEL 06(373)2411

– You may find it surprising that there are hardly any **street names** and no **house numbers**.
– **You can easily get lost!** To avoid this, here are three helpful tips:

1 Each institution, every store and nearly every person has a little card to help you find your way. The position of the house or building is illustrated in relation to stations, well-known streets, parks etc.

2. You can ask the police or passers-by for the directions. Policemen consider this service to be an important part of their duty.

3. Telephone the person whose home you are trying to find and ask him to describe the way.

At all events, ask the desk clerk of your hotel to write down your destination in Japanese and also ask him for a card showing the way to your hotel.

1 Air **2** Urban transport **3** Rail **4** Ship

5.1	空港	kūkō	airport
	東京（成田）		Tokyo (Narita)
	ゲート	gēto	gate
	便	bin	flight
	便名	bin-mei	flight number (= flight-name)
	国際線	kokūsai-sen	international flights
	国内線	kokūnai-sen	domestic flights
	日本航空	Nihon-kōkū	Japan Air Lines
	航空券	kōkū-ken	aeroplane ticket
	出発	shuppatsu	departure
	到着	tōchaku	arrival

5.2	バス	basu	bus
	タクシー	takushī	taxi
	地下鉄	chiká-tetsu	underground
			(= earth-below-iron)
	のりかえ	norikae	transfer, change

空港へ行って下さい。 kūkō-e itte kudasái.	To the airport, please (= Airport-to drive please.)
地下鉄の駅はどこですか。 chiká-tetsu-no eki-wa 　doko desu ka?	Where is the underground 　station? (= Underground- 　*genitive* station-*subject* 　where be *interrogative*.)

5 Public Transport

5.3	鉄道	tetsu-do	railway (= iron-street)
	国鉄	koku-tetsu	national railways (JNR); also called koku-den, JR (jei-āru) or JR-sen.
	私鉄	shi-tetsu	private railway (= I-railway)
	電車	densha	electric train
	駅	eki	station
	のりば	noribá	platform
	線	sen	line
	新幹線	shin-kan-sen	Bullet Train (*high-speed train*)
	グリーン車	grin-sha	first-class carriage (= green-car)
	禁煙車	kin-en-sha	no smoking carriage
	うち	uchi	aisle
	内側	uchigawa	aisle seat
	まど	mado	window
	窓側	madogawa	window seat
	案内所	annaisho	information
	予約	yoyaku	reservation
	切符	kippu	ticket

広島行の切符を一枚下さい。 A ticket to Hiroshima, please.
Hiroshima-yuki-no
  kippu-o ichimai kudasái.

(= Hiroshima-to-*genitive* ticket-*direct-object* one-piece please.)

いくらですか。 How much is it?
ikura desu ka?

(= How-much be *interrogative*.)

新宿行きはどれですか。 Which is the train to Shinjuku?
Shinjuku yuki-wa dore
  desu ka?

(= Shinjuku direction-*subject* which be *interrogative*.)

5.4	港	minato	port
	フェリー	ferī	ferry
	船	fune	boat, ship

1. Tell the taxi driver you would like to go to the airport:
. . . .

You are at Osaka airport. Which signs do you look for?

2. You're looking for 'Departures': . . . .

3. You're looking for 'Domestic flights':

   . . . .

4. You're flying abroad: . . . .

5. You are in Tokyo and you can't find the suburban-line station. You ask a policeman or a passer-by:

   . . . .

6. You can't find your way in the station. You ask where the train to SHINJUKU leaves from:

   . . . .

You want to go from Osaka to Hiroshima by Shinkansen.

7. You would like a ticket:

   . . . .

8. First class: . . . .

9. You ask for a window seat: . . . .

10. What is the word for 'ticket' in Japanese?

    . . . .

5 Public Transport

11. What do you call this kind of boat?

. . . .

- In Tokyo the **underground** and **suburban trains** are quick and inexpensive ways to travel. Try to obtain a general map.

- You get **tickets** from vending machines. A general map shows you the fare; these maps are often only written in Japanese.

- The **names of many stations** are not only written in Japanese but also in Latin letters (small characters). The name of the next station is usually given as well.

- Each tube line has its own **name** and special **colour**.

- In high-speed trains (**Shinkansen**) most carriages have reserved seats. Do book in time! You will recognise first-class carriages by a green cloverleaf.

- **Narita airport** is 40 miles from Tokyo, about an hour away by car or bus. Take the limousine-bus, which stops right in front of the airport.

- The **airport tax** of 2000 yen has to be paid before departing from Tokyo-Narita.

1 Hotel **2** Rooms **3** Prices **4** Toilets

6.1	ホテル	hoteru	hotel
	旅館	ryokan	hotel (*Japanese-style*) (= travelling-building)
6.2	フロント	furonto	reception desk
	予約	yoyaku	reservation (= before-promise)
	部屋	heya	room (= part-of-the-house)
	鍵／カギ	kagi	key
	エレベーター	erebētā	lift
	1階／1 F	ikkai	ground floor, main floor
	2階／2 F	nikai	second floor up – i.e. first floor
	非常口	hijōguchi	emergency exit

予約しました。 yoyaku shimashita.	I've made a reservation. (= Reservation have-made.)
一人用の部屋を下さい。 hitóri-yō-no heya-o kudasái.	A single room, please. (= One-person-for-*genitive* room-*direct-object* please.)

6 Accommodation

二人用の部屋を下さい。　　A double room, please.
futari-yō-no heya-o kudasái.　(= Two-persons-for-*genitive*
　　　　　　　　　　　　　　　room-*direct-object* please.)

1泊/2泊　　　　　　　　　For one night / for two
ippaku / nihaku　　　　　　nights.

鍵を下さい。　　　　　　　The key, please.
kagi-o kudasái.　　　　　　(= Key-*direct-object* please.)

6.3　フロント会計　furonto-kaikei　cashier (at reception)
　　　勘定　　　　kanjō　　　　　bill

部屋代はいくらですか。　　How much is the room?
heya-dai wa ikura desu ka?　(= Room-*subject* how-much
　　　　　　　　　　　　　　be *interrogative*.)

お勘定を下さい。　　　　　The bill, please.
o-kanjō-o kudasái.　　　　(= *Polite-prefix*-bill-*direct-
　　　　　　　　　　　　　object* please.)

6.4　トイレ　　　　　tóire　　　　　toilets
　　　男性　　　　　dansei　　　　Gentlemen
　　　女性　　　　　josei　　　　　Ladies
　　　石けん　　　　sekken　　　　soap
　　　ベッド　　　　beddo　　　　　bed
　　　電気カミソリ　denki kamisori　razor

トイレはどこですか。　　　Where are the toilets?
tóire-wa doko desu ka?　　(= Toilets-*subject* where be
　　　　　　　　　　　　　　interrogative.)

トイレが流れません。　　　The toilet doesn't flush.
tóire-ga nagare masen.　　(= *Toilet-subject* work-not.)

What are these called in Japanese?

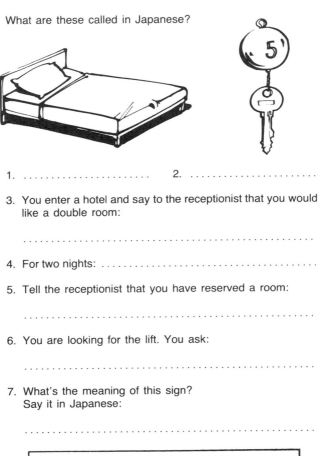

1. . . . .   2. . . . .

3. You enter a hotel and say to the receptionist that you would like a double room:

   . . . .

4. For two nights: . . . .

5. Tell the receptionist that you have reserved a room:

   . . . .

6. You are looking for the lift. You ask:

   . . . .

7. What's the meaning of this sign?
   Say it in Japanese:

   . . . .

6 Accommodation

What are these called in Japanese?

8. .... 9. ....

10. You want to know where the toilets are.
    You ask:

    ....

- The **international hotels** are excellent, but very expensive.

- The traditional Japanese **ryokan-hotels** are rarely equipped to accommodate foreign tourists. One sleeps of 'futon' cushions laid out on 'tatami' floors.

- The voltage is **100 volts**.

- There are many 'Japanese-style' **toilets**: You squat above the small basin, facing the wall.

1 Numbers **2** Counting

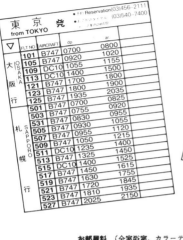

お部屋料 （全室浴室、カラーテレビ、冷暖房完備）

	お 1 人 様	お 2 人 様
お 1 人 室	¥ 4,000 ¥ 4,200 ¥ 4,400	
お 2 人 室	¥ 4,200 ¥ 4,400 ¥ 6,000	¥ 6,400 ¥ 6,600 ¥ 8,000
和 室	¥ 6,000	¥ 8,000

7.1

一	1	ichi	十	10	jū	19	jū-kyū/jū-ku
二	2	ni		11	jū-ichi	20	ni-jū
三	3	san		12	jū-ni	30	san-jū
四	4	shi (yon)		13	jū-san	40	yon-jū
五	5	go		14	jū-shi	50	go-jū
六	6	roku			(ju-yon)	60	roku-jū
七	7	shichi		15	jū-go	70	nana-jū
		(nana)		16	jū-roku	80	hachi-jū
八	8	hachi		17	jū-nana/jūshichi	90	kyū-jū
九	9	kyū		18	jū-hachi	百 100	hyaku

7 Numbers and Counting

200	ni-hyaku	5,000	go-sen
300	sam-byaku*	8,000	has-sen*
500	go-hyaku	一万 10,000	ichi-man
600	rop-pyaku*	100,000	yū-man
800	hap-pyaku*	1,000,000	hyaku-man
千 1,000	sen		

百円	hyaku en	100 Yen
五千円	go-sen en	5,000 Yen

7.2

つ	-tsu	piece (*counting objects*)
枚	-mai	piece (*counting thin things like paper, records, stamps, clothes*)
台	-dai	piece (*counting machines, cars*)
冊	-satsu	piece (*counting books*)
本	-bon / hon	piece (*counting bottles and other long, cylindrical objects*)

一つ hitotsu	one piece
二つ futatsu	two pieces
三つ mittsu	three pieces
四つ yottsu...	four pieces...
コーヒーを一つ下さい。 Kōhī-o hitotsu kudasai.	One coffee, please. (= Coffee-*direct-object* one-piece please.)
一枚 ichimai	one piece
二枚 nimai...	two pieces...
切手を五枚下さい。 Kitte-o go-mai kudasai.	Five stamps, please. (= Stamps-*direct-object* five-pieces please.)

* *Assimilation for better pronunciation.*

Which rooms are these hotel guests staying in?

1. Mr Tanaka: . . . .   2. Mr Tagaki: . . . .

3. Mr Miller: . . . .   4. Mr Smith: . . . .

Look at this boarding pass.

Say in Japanese

5. . . .the flight number: . . . .

6. . . .the day: . . . .

7. . . .the seat number: . . . .

7 Numbers and Counting

Look at this underground ticket.

8. How much did it cost?

....

Look at this ticket for
the Hiroshima Peace
Museum.

9. How much did it cost?

....

B № 170684

広 島 平 和
記念資料館

観 覧 券

(有効当日限り)

大人券 ¥50

- Learning Japanese **numbers** is not difficult: With the help
  of 13 words you can derive all numbers up to 1,000,000.

- Notice that there is a special word for 10,000: man.

- **4** is considered to be an unlucky number. 4(shi) sounds
  just like the word for 'death': 死

- For weights and measures the Japanese use the **metric
  system**:

1 inch = 2.54 cm		1 gallon = 3.785 l
1 foot = 30.48 cm		1 barrel = 159.106 l
1 yard = 91.44 cm		1 ounce = 28.35 g
1 mile = 1.609 km		1 pound = 353.59 g

---

1 Time   **2** Time of day   **3** Days and dates

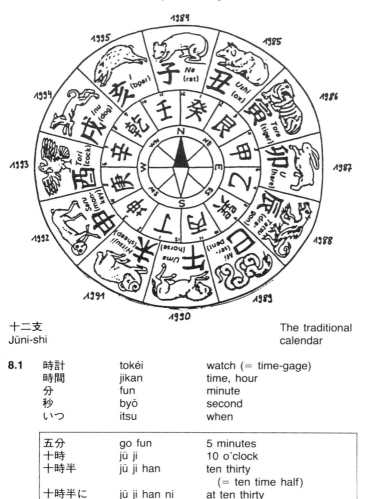

十二支
Jūni-shi

The traditional
calendar

8.1	時計	tokéi	watch (= time-gage)
	時間	jikan	time, hour
	分	fun	minute
	秒	byō	second
	いつ	itsu	when

五分	go fun	5 minutes
十時	jū ji	10 o'clock
十時半	jū ji han	ten thirty
		(= ten time half)
十時半に	jū ji han ni	at ten thirty
		(= ten time half at)

8 Times and Dates

8.2

日	hi	day, sun
朝	asa ⎫	morning, in the morning
午前	go-zen ⎭	(= noon-earlier)
午後	go-go	afternoon, in the afternoon
夕方	yū-gata	late in the afternoon
夜	yoru	evening, night
今日	kyō	today (= now-day)
昨日	kinō	yesterday
明日	ashita	tomorrow

朝八時	asa hachi ji	eight o'clock in the morning.
一寸待って下さい。	chotto matte kudasái.	One moment, please.

8.3

週	shū	week
月曜日	getsu-yōbi	Monday (= moon-day)
火曜日	ka-yōbi	Tuesday (= fire-day)
水曜日	sui-yōbi	Wednesday (= water-day)
木曜日	moku-yōbi	Thursday (= wood-day)
金曜日	kin-yōbi	Friday (gold-day)
土曜日	do-yōbi	Saturday (= earth-day)
日曜日	nichi-yōbi	Sunday (= sun-day)
年	toshi	year
月	gatsu, tsuki	month, moon
一月	ichi gatsu	January (= 1 month)
二月	ni gatsu	February (= 2 month)
三月	san gatsu...	March (= 3 month)...

3月31日	san gatsu san-jū ichi nichi	31 March (= 3 month 31 day)

Say in Japanese:

1. 60 seconds are 1 . . . .

2. 60 minutes are 1 . . . .

3. 24 hours are 1 ....

4. 7 days are 1 ....

5. 12 months are 1 ....

6. What is this? Say it in Japanese:

....

[12:35 watch]

What time is it?

7. ....

8. ....

9. ....

10. ....

8 Times and Dates

What do these symbols/characters stand for in Japanese and what is their English translation?

11. ☼ → ◉ → ⊟ → 日   Jap.: . . . .
                          Engl.: . . . .

12. 🐇 → ☾ → 𠃜 → 月   Jap.: . . . .
                          Engl.: . . . .

- The Japanese first give the time of day – morning, afternoon or evening – and then the hour.

- Instead of **fun** (= minute) you say: 1/3/4/6/8/10 **pun** (for easier pronounciation).

- It's easy to form the names of the **months:** January = 1 month, February = 2 month, etc.

- Some **time differences:**

Auckland	+ 3 hours	Moscow	– 6 hours
Sydney	+ 1 hour	Frankfurt, Paris, Rome	– 8 hours
Peking, Hong Kong, Manila	– 1 hour	London	– 9 hours
Bangkok	– 2 hours	New York, Montreal	– 14 hours
New Delhi	– 4 hours	San Francisco	– 17 hours

 Tokyo | 8 hrs |

San Francisco
| 15 hrs |

Frankfurt, Paris, Rome
| 24 hrs |

New York, Montreal | 18 hrs | London | 23 hrs |

42

1 Currency **2** Changing money **3** Shops
4 Prices

maneki-neko
招き猫

The cat is a good luck charm
in business.

9.1

お金	o-kane	money
円（¥）	en	yen
ポンド	pondo	pound(s)
ドル	doru	dollar(s)

千円	sen en	1,000 yen
五千円	go-sen en	5,000 yen
五万円	go-man en	50,000 yen

9.2

銀行	ginkō	bank (= silver- corporation)
両替	ryōgae	exchange

9 Money

両替はどこでできますか。	Where is there an exchange bureau?
ryōgae-wa doko de dekimasu ka?	(= Exchange-*subject* where possible be *interrogative*.)
百ポンドを両替して下さい。	I'd like to change £100, please.
hyaku pondo-o ryōgae shite kudasái.	(= 100 pounds-*direct-object* change make please.)

9.3

店	mise	shop, store
売店	baiten	kiosk, stand
デパート	depāto	department store
スーパー	sūpā	supermarket
セルフサービス	serufu sābisu	self-service
本日休業	hónjitsu kyūgyō	closing day

9.4

値段/ねだん	nedan	price (= price-level)
高い	takai	expensive
割引	waribiki	discount price
免税店	menzeiten	tax-free shop
勘定	kanjō	bill
お勘定場	o-kanjōba	cash-desk (= *polite-prefix*-bill-place)

これはいくらですか。	How much is it?
(kore-wa)ikura desu ka?	(= it-*subject* how-much be *interrogative*.)
書いて下さい。	Would you write it down, please?
kaite kudasái.	(= Write please.)
これは高いです。	That's expensive.
kore-wa takái desu.	(= That-*subject* expensive be.)
領収証を下さい。	I'd like a receipt, please.
ryōshūshō-o kudasái.	(= Receipt-*direct-object* please.)

In the following spaces you can write approximate current exchange rates:

10 ¥ =	....	1,000 ¥ =	....
100 ¥ =	....	5,000 ¥ =	....
500 ¥ =	....	10,000 ¥ =	....

You want to change some money.

1. You are looking for a bank. Which sign do you look for?

   ....

2. You enter the bank and ask where you can change money:

   ....

3. You would like to change £100. You say:

   ....

In a shop. You would like to pay.

4. You ask the salesperson how much you have to pay:

   ....

5. You haven't understood the price and ask him or her to write it down:

   ....

6. In Japanese a discount is called:

   ....

9 Money

How much did the customer pay

7. for a book?

. . . .

8. for three items?

. . . .

```
┌──────────────────┐
│  田村書店         │
│  TEL 291-0563    │
│                  │
│  ¥ 300           │
│                  │
└──────────────────┘
```

```
┌──────────────────┐
│  ◆ 伊縁义         │
│  ﾀﾜｰ店 TEL 371-0925│
│                  │
│  60-08-15        │
│  #00             │
│  I       750     │
│  I       500     │
│  I       500     │
│        1,750     │
└──────────────────┘
```

- **Opening hours:**

	weekdays	Saturdays	Sundays, holidays
banks (Closed every weekend.)	9:00–15:00	9:00–12:00	closed
post offices	9:00–17:00	9:00–12:30	closed
department stores	10:00–18:00 (Closed one weekday.)	10:00–18:30	10:00–18:30
other stores	10:00–20:00	10:00–20:00	10:00–20:00

- Bargaining over an item is not customary in Japan. However, looking around in different shops and districts to compare prices is to be recommended.

- You always **pay cash**.

- It is possible to cash **traveller's checks** in banks and hotels.

- In Japan it's not customary to leave **tips**.

1 Souvenirs **2** Clothes **3** Electrical / electronic goods

10.1	漆器	shikki	lacquer ware
	陶器	tōki	pottery
	人形	ningyō	doll (= man-look-like)
	達磨	daruma	happy doll
	真珠	shinjú	pearls
	骨董品	kottōhin	antiques
	うちわ	uchiwa	fan

10 Shopping in Japan

10.2

洋服	yō-fuku	Western-style garments
ブラウス	burausu	blouse
シャツ	shatsu	shirt
セーター	sētā	pullover, sweater
着物	ki-mono	kimono (= put-on-thing)
絹	kinu	silk
ウール	ūru	wool
コットン	kotton	cotton
靴	kutsu	shoes

10.3

電子器具	denshi-kigu	electronic equipment
ラジオ	rajio	radio
トランジスター	toranjisutā	transistor
ステレオ	sutereo	stereo set
レコード	rekōdo	record
カセット	kasetto	cassette
コンピューター	kompyūtā	computer
マイコン	maikon	microcomputer
パソコン	pasokon	personal computer
ソフトウエア	sofutouea	software
ポケット計算器	poketto keisanki	pocket calculator
腕時計	ude-dokei	watch

カメラを買いたい。 Kamera-o kaitai.	I want to buy a camera. (= Camera-*direct-object* want-to-buy.)
…はありますか。 ...-wa arimásu ka?	Do you have ...? (= ...-*subject* there-is *interrogative*.)
これを見せて下さい。 kore-o misete kudasái.	Would you show me this, please (= This-*direct-object* show please.)
これを下さい。 kore-o kudasái	I'll take this. (= This-*direct-object* take.)

You are in a store and ask the salesperson if he has the following items:

2. . . . .

3. . . . .

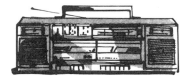

1. . . . .   4. . . . .

5. . . . .   6. . . . .

10 Shopping in Japan

7. You see a lovely lacquer bowl in the showcase and ask the sales-person to show it to you: . . . .

8. After having had a close look at the bowl you would like to buy it.
   You say: . . . .

- There are huge **department stores** in Tokyo and in other cities, e.g. Isetan, Matsuya, Mitsukoshi, Seibu, Tokyu.

- The main **shopping areas** in Tokyo are Ginza 銀座 and Shinjuku 新宿 in the West.

- The electric and electronic equipment shopping district is in Akihabara 秋葉原, 1 mile north of Tokyo Central Station 東京駅.

- In many stores you can **buy** jewellery (especially pearls), furs, cameras and lenses, watches, microcomputers etc. **tax-free** and get a discount of 5% to 40%. When you purchase something tax-free, a form is placed in your passport which you have to show with the tax-free goods at the customs when leaving the country.

- The traditional ladies' wear is the **kimono**, which can be seen in beautiful displays in department stores. However, you will rarely see them being worn on the street.

Women's Dresses & Suits

Japanese	9	11	13	15	17	19	21
English	32	34	36	38	40	42	44
Continental	38	40	42	44	46	48	50
American	10	12	14	16	18	20	22

Men's Suits, Overcoats & Sweaters

Japanese	S		M		L		LL
English	34	36	38	40	42	44	46
Continental	44	46	48	50	52	54	56
American	34	36	38	40	42	44	46

1 Meals **2** Tableware **3** Breakfast **4** Snacks

Hold one chop-stick between your thumb and middle finger, so that the middle part of it rests on your ring finger just beside the fingernail.

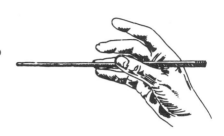

Place the second chop-stick between your index finger and your middle finger like a pencil and press it hard with your thumb.

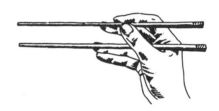

The bottom chop-stick does not move while the top one is moved lightly to pick up the food.

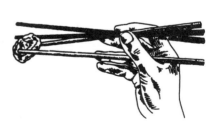

11.1	食	shoku	eat, appetite
	食事	shokuji	meals (= eat-matter)
	朝食	chōshoku	breakfast
	昼食	chūshoku	lunch
	夕食	yūshoku	dinner, supper

11 Meals

11.2

カップ	kappu	cup
グラス	gurasu	glass
皿	sara	plate, dish
スプーン	supūn	spoon
フォーク	fōku	fork
ナイフ	naifu	knife
おはし	o-hashi	chop-sticks

フォークを下さい。	A fork, please.
fōku-o kudasái.	(= Fork-*direct-object* please.)

11.3

パン	pan	bread
トースト	tōsuto	toast
バター	batā	butter
ジャム	jamu	jam
タマゴ	tamago	egg (= ball-child)
コーヒー	kōhī	coffee
お茶	o-cha	tea
ミルク	miruku	milk
ヨーグルト	yōguruto	yoghurt

11.4

軽食	keishoku	snack (= light-meal)
寿司/鮨/すし	sushi	raw fish with vegetables and vinegar-seasoned rice
サンドイッチ	sandoittchi	sandwich
ハム	hamu	ham
ベーコン	bēkon	bacon

What are the three meals of the day called in Japanese?

1. In the morning: ....

2. At noon: ....

3. In the evening: ....

What are the following called in Japanese?

4. .... 5. ....

6. .... 7. ....

8. .... 9. ....

10. ....

11. You do not know how to eat with chop-sticks.
    You ask the waiter for a fork:

    ....

11 Meals

12. What is this typical Japanese meal called?

....

- **Sushi** is the most popular snack in Japan. In Tokyo alone there are more than 7,000 sushi-restaurants. Sushi is made of small portions of vinegar-seasoned rice with slices of raw fish.
- If you don't care for **Japanese** food, you don't have to go hungry, because you are able to order both Japanese and western food. The largest chain of fast-food restaurants in Japan is McDonald's.
- You can safety eat and drink everything in Japan.

1 Eating places **2** Service **3** Seasonings
4 The bill

12 Restaurants

12.1
レストラン	résutoran	restaurant
喫茶店	kissaten	tea shop, café
食堂	shokudō	canteen

12.2
テーブル	tēburu	table
畳	tatami	'tatami' mat (*made of rice straw*)
食券	shokken	meal coupons
メニュー	ményū	menu

これを下さい。 Kore-o kudasái.	I'd like this...* (= This-*direct-object* please.)
これはいくらですか。 Kore-wa ikura desu ka?	How much is it? (= It-*subject* how-much be *interrogative*.)

12.3
塩	shio	salt
砂糖	satō	sugar (= sand-sugar)
コショウ	koshō	pepper
酢	su	vinegar
みりん	mirin	sweet rice wine (*for cooking*)
出し/だし	dashi	fish broth, fish stock (*for fish, vegetables, noodles*)
醤油	shōyu	soy sauce
生姜	shōga	ginger

12.4
ウエイター	ueitā	waiter
ウエイトレス	ueitoresu	waitress
支払い	shiharái	paying

お勘定をおねがいします。 o-kanjō-o onegaishimasu	I'd like the bill, please. (= *Polite-prefix*-check-*direct-object* want-to-make.)

*You point to the plastic replica (see p. 58).

Where can you eat?

1. You want a snack:

   . . . .

2. You are looking for the restaurant in a department store:

   . . . .

3. You want to have dinner:

   . . . .

You choose your meal.

4. You take the waitress to the display-case and show her what
   you want to eat.

   You say to her: . . . .

5. You want to know how much it costs.

   You ask her: . . . .

What is in these containers?

6. . . . .   7. . . . .   8. . . . .

9. You would like to pay. You say to the waitress:

   . . . .

12 Restaurants

- In Japan you will find a great variety of **restaurants**, serving native Japanese specialties and international cuisine.

- Dummy meals are shown in plastic in the **display-cases** of the restaurants.

- For a Japanese not only the taste of the meal is of great importance, but also **presentation**.

- **Department stores** serve inexpensive and tasty meals.

- Before the meal you are given a damp flannel in a sealed plastic bag with which you can wipe your face and your hands.

- Ocha, the customary Japanese **green tea** (never drunk with sugar or milk) is served with each meal.

- Many restaurants have an area with tables and chairs and another in Japanese style (where the guests take off their shoes and kneel on cushions on the 'tatami').

- You do not pay the waiter, but at the cash-desk which is located by the exit. At many places you must buy **coupons** (shokken) before sitting down, and the waitress will bring you the meal. If you would like an additional helping, you return to the cash-desk and buy another meal coupon.

- In spite of the good service, people do not give any **tips**.

- **Soy sauce** is a typical Japanese seasoning for all occasions. 80% of all dishes are flavoured with it. Soy sauce is made of cooked soya beans and roasted wheat. The fermentation process takes 6 months. – Soy sauce can only be stored for a limited time.

1 Starters **2** Meat **3** Poultry, eggs **4** Fish

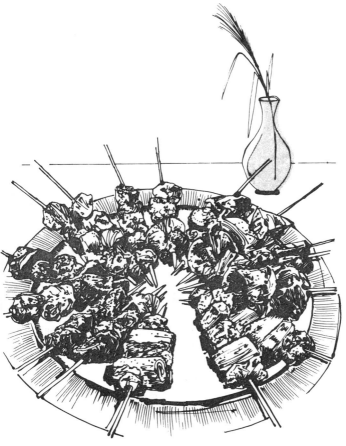

13.1	お通し	o-tōshi	appetisers
	スープ	sūpu	soup, broth
	そば	soba	buckwheat noodles
	うどん	udon	white noodles (*thicker than 'soba', made of wheat flour*)

13 Noodles, Meat, Fish

13.2

肉	niku	meat
すき焼き	sukiyaki	dish of thinly-sliced beef, vegetables, tofu, egg and soy sauce (*cooked at the table*)
とんかつ	tonkatsu	pork chop (= pork-'to cut')
レバー	rebā	liver

13.3

やきとり	yakitori	skewers of grilled pieces of chicken, liver, onion, etc. (= fried-chicken)
もも	mómo	chicken drumstick
タマゴ	tamago	egg (= ball-child)
タマゴドン	tamago-don	bowl of cooked rice and omelet

13.4

魚	sakana	fish
まぐろ	maguro	tuna
うなぎ	unagi	eel
かつお	katsuo	bonito (*fish*)
えび	ebi	shrimp, prawn
刺身	sáshimi	sliced raw fish served with soy sauce dip
天ふら	tempura	shellfish, prawns, vegetables, seaweed coated in light batter and fried in oil
おでん	oden	dish of fish cakes, tofu, radish, eggs, etc.
盛合せ	moriawase	assorted plate or bowl of food

1. What is this Japanese lady eating?

. . . .

or

. . . .

What are these called?

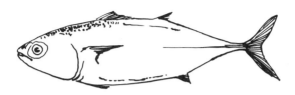

2. (tuna): . . . .

3. (bonito): . . . .

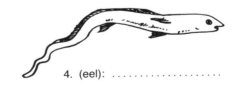

4. (eel): . . . .

5. (shrimp): . . . .

13 Noodles, Meat, Fish

6. What is the Japanese dish on page 59 called?

. . . .

Have a look at this meal coupon (shokken):

タマゴドン

·PU¥·600

7. What was ordered? . . . .

8. How much did it cost? . . . .

- **Noodles** are an inexpensive fast food. 'Soba' are grey and made of buckwheat.
- The Japanese way to eat noodles is to 'slurp' them loudly.
- Japanese enjoy **seafood** very much, e.g. sliced raw fish: sashimi.
- Japanese cuisine has two kinds of **soups**: clear dashi-broth (made of fish) and miso-soup (made of soya bean paste).
- Grilled or cooked **eel** (unagi) served with a sweet sauce is a delicacy.
- You pay for **yakitori** according to the number of skewers you have consumed.
- **Meat**, especially steak, is very expensive in Japan.
- A special delicacy is **globe-fish** (fugu) which is poisonous if the innards are not carefully removed. Chefs must have a licence to prepare this speciality.

---

1 Vegetables **2** Fruit **3** Desserts

14 Vegetables, Fruit, Desserts

14.1

野菜	yasai	vegetables (= field-food)
大豆	daizu	soya bean (= big bean)
豆腐	tōfu	soya bean curd
みそ	miso	soya bean paste (*seasoning*)
玉ねぎ	tamanegi	onion (= ball-leek)
にんじん	ninjin	carrot
大根	daikon	radish (= big root)
竹の子	takenoko	bamboo shoots
米	komé	raw rice
ご飯	gohan	cooked rice
丼	dómburi	bowl of cooked rice
のり	nori	(*for wrapping small balls of rice*)
こんぶ	kombu	*seaweed* (*for broth*)
わかめ	wakame	(*in the soup*)

14.2

りんご	ringo	apple
オレンジ	orenji	orange
バナナ	banana	banana

14.3

デザート	dezāto	dessert
氷	kōri	both ordinary ice and flavoured shaved ice
イチゴ	ichigo	strawberry (red)
メロン	meron	melon (green)
レモン	remon	lemon (yellow)
アイスクリーム	aisukurīmu	ice-cream
バニラ	banira	vanilla
チョコレート	chokorēto	chocolate
クッキー	kukkī	biscuit(s)

What are the following called in Japanese?

1. . . . .   2. . . . .

3. . . . .   4. . . . .

5. . . . .   6. . . . .

7. What can you buy
when you see
this sign?

. . . .

14 Vegetables, Fruit, Desserts

8. You want to have a strawberry-flavoured shaved ice.

   You say to the seller: ....

9. You want to have melon-flavoured shaved ice.

   You say to the seller: ....

10. You want to buy some ice-cream; you would like vanilla.

    You say to the seller: ....

- Japanese **rice** becomes tender and glutinous when it is cooked, making it easy to eat with chop-sticks. It is cooked without seasoning and is an essential part of every Japanese meal.

- **Seaweed** is low in calories, but it contains a lot of iodine and carotin.

- Soya bean curd (**tōfu**) is a staple food in Japan. It is low in calories and contains high-quality protein and calcium. It has no flavour and can be fried, cooked or grilled.

- The Japanese like **cakes**, **biscuits** and **sweets** of all kinds; they buy them in large, attractive boxes.

1 Non-alcoholic drinks   2 Alcoholic drinks
3 Smoking

15.1	コーヒー	kōhī	coffee (*very strong*)
	アメリカン	amerikan	American coffee
	お茶	o-cha	green tea (= *polite-prefix-tea*)
	紅茶	kōcha	tea (= red tea)
	水	mizu	plain tap water
	（コカ）コーラ	(koka-)kōra	coca cola
	ジュース	jūsu	juice
	リンゴジュース	ringo-jūsu	apple juice
	オレンジジュース	orenji-jūsu	orange juice

15 Drinking and Smoking

（コカ）コーラを1つ下さい。 (koka-)kōra-o hitotsu kudasái.	A coke, please. (= Coca Cola-*direct-object* one-piece please.)	
お茶を下さい。 o-cha-o kudasái.	Tea, please. (= *Polite-prefix-tea-direct-object* please.)	
水を下さい。 mizu-o kudasái.	Water, please. (= Water-*direct-object* please.)	

15.2

酒	sake	rice wine
清酒	sei-shu	special quality rice wine
梅酒	ume-shu	plum wine
ビール	bīru	beer
ウイスキー	uisukī	whisky
ブランデー	burándē	brandy
瓶/びん	bin	bottle

ビールを1本下さい。 bīru-o ippon* kudasái.	A beer, please. (= Beer-*direct-object* one-piece please.)	
ビールを2本下さい。 bīru-o nihon* kudasái.	Two beers, please. (= Beer-*direct-object* two-pieces please.)	
乾杯　Kampai!	Cheers!	

15.3

たばこ	tábako	cigarette
マッチ	mattchi	matches
灰皿	haizara	ashtray (= ash-plate)

* Or: bīru-o hitotsu (*one beer*) / futatsu (*two beers*) ...

タバコをひとつ下さい。
tabako-o hitotsu kudasái.
	A packet of cigarettes,
	   please.
	(= Cigarettes-*direct-
	   object* one-piece
	   please.)

禁煙 kin-en	No smoking.

MENU
ロマンスカービュッフェ

★喫 茶		★酒 類	
コ ー ヒ ー Coffee	330	ビール(中) Bottled Beer(M)	470
アイスコーヒー Ice Coffee (4/21~11/5)	350	ナマ樽ビール(1.2ℓ)(4/21~10/31)	1,300
紅 茶 Tea Cream or Lemon	330	日 本 酒 Japanese Sake	300
アイスクリーム Ice Cream	220	梅酒(チューヤ) Plum Wine	280
オレンジジュース Orange Juice	260	スコッチウイスキー(50mℓ・水付) Findlater's	680
コ カ・コ ー ラ Coca-Cola	260	サントリーオールド(50mℓ・水付) Suntory Whisky	600

Order the following from this bilingual menu:

1. A coke: . . . .

2. A beer: . . . .

3. An orange juice: . . . .

4. What is contained in the
   cup and bottle?

   . . . .

15 Drinking and Smoking

5. You are very thirsty and would like some water before the meal. You say to the waiter:

. . . .

6. You would like some green tea.

You say: . . . .

. . . .

7. You want to buy some cigarettes. Which sign do you look for?

. . . .

- **Sake** is a clear and mild drink which contains 15 to 17% alcohol. Traditionally served warm, it can also be ordered as a cold drink during the summer.

- Japanese **beer** is internationally popular.

- In comparison with American coffee, Japanese **coffee** is strong and expensive.

---

1 Tourism **2** Attractions **3** Traditional arts
4 Admission

16.1	観光	kankō	tourism, sightseeing
	観光客	kankō-kyaku	tourist (= sightseeing-guest)
	ガイド	gaido	guide
	団体	dantai	group
	パンフレット	panfuretto	brochure, pamphlet

16 Sightseeing

| パンフレットを1枚下さい。
panfuretto-o ichimai kudasái. | A brochure, please.
(= Brochure *direct-object*
one-piece please.) |

16.2

天皇	tennō	Tenno (= heaven-emperor)
皇届	kōkyo	emperor's palace
皇后	kōgō	empress
神道	shintō	Shinto (*Japanese religion*)
神宮	jingū	big Shinto shrine (= temple)
神社	jinja	Shinto shrine
鳥居	torii	gate (*to the Shinto shrine*)
仏	hotoke	Buddha
大仏	daibutsu	great Buddha
仏像	butsuzō	statue of the Buddha
寺	tera	Buddhist temple
城	shiro	castle
博物館	hakubútsu-kan	museum (= conserve- things-building)

東京国立博物館	Tokyō kokuritsu hakubútsu-kan	Tokyo National Museum
金閣寺	kinkakuji	Golden Pavilion (*temple in Kyoto*)
名古屋城	Nagoya-jo	Castle of Nagoya

16.3

歌舞伎	kabuki	traditional play
能	nō	classical drama (*with music and dance*)
相撲	sumō	Japanese wrestling
柔道	jūdō	judo

16.4

入館料	nyūkan-ryō	admission charge
入口	iriguchi	entrance
出口	deguchi	exit
押す	osu	push
引く	hiku	pull

Do you recognise these Japanese tourist attractions?

(Castle of Nagoya)

(Golden Pavilion)

1. ....

2. ....

(Great Buddha)

(Gate)

3. ....

4. ....

5. What does this sign indicate?

....

16 Sightseeing

6. In which traditional theatrical art does this actor participate?

....

7. What is this sport called?

....

- In Tokyo there are many public and private **museums**. The most important of these are in the Ueno-Park (National Museum/kokuritsu hakubutskan). They are open from 9 a.m. to at least 4 p.m.

- Before you enter a temple or a castle you must **take off your shoes**.

- If you want to go out for a night on the town, you should be with an organised group or accompanied by a Japanese. In many bars only Japanese or 'members' are admitted.

- The traditional Japanese **wrestling** sport is called 'sumo', whose participants have to weigh at least 280 pounds. If the wrestler is pushed out of the ring or touches the ground, he has lost the match. The arena is by the suburban-line station Ryogoku.

1 Scenery **2** Gardens and flowers **3** Photography

富士山

17.1	海	umi	sea, ocean
	島	shima	island
	川	kawa	river
	山	-san, yama	mountain
	富士山	fujisan	Mount Fuji
			(= rich-man-mountain)
	火山	kazan	volcano (= fire-mountain)
	地震	jishin	earthquake

17 Countryside, Photography

17.2

-園	-en	garden
公園	kōen	park (= public-garden)
花	hana	flower
生け花	ikebana	flower arranging (= flowers-make-living)
桜	sakura	cherry blossom
菊	kiku	chrysanthemum
松	matsu	pine tree
盆栽	bonsai	bonsai (*miniature trees*)

17.3

カメラ	kámera	camera
レンズ	renzu	lens
望遠レンズ	bōen-renzu	telephoto lens
電池	denchi	battery
フラッシュ	furasshu	flash
フィルム	firumu	film
写真	sha-shin	photo (= copy-real)
スライド	suraido	slide
カメラ店	kamera-ten	photo shop

フィルムを一つ下さい。
firumu-o hitotsu kudasái.

A film, please.
(= Film-*direct-object* one-piece please.)

カメラを買いたい。
kamera-o kaitai.

I want to buy a camera.
(= Camera-*direct-object* want-to-buy.)

What do these symbols stand for in Japanese and what are their English translations?

1.

→ 山

Jap.: . . . .

Engl.: . . . .

2.

→ 川

Jap.: . . . .

Engl.: . . . .

3. What mountain can you see on the bank note?

. . . .

4. Which tree can you see in the foreground?

. . . .

5. What are these miniature trees called?

. . . .

17 Countryside, Photography

What are these objects called in Japanese?

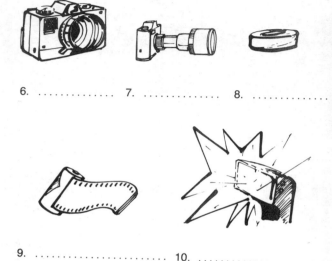

6. .... 7. .... 8. ....

9. .... 10. ....

- Every year there are more than 1,000 small **earth-quakes** in Japan. During the last great earthquake in September 1923 more than 200,000 people were killed in Tokyo.

- Conduct during an earthquake:
  1. Keep calm! Don't leave the house panic-stricken because you could be injured by breaking glass, etc.
  2. Open a door or a window in order to be near an exit after the earthquake.
  3. Look for shelter (e.g. hide under a table!).
  4. The underground and underground shopping centres are considered to be earthquake-proof.

1 The weather **2** Good **3** Bad **4** Cold weather

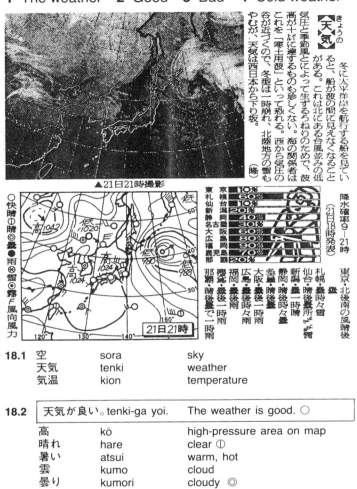

▲21日21時撮影

冬に太平洋岸を航行する船を見ていると、船が波の間に見えなくなることがある。これは北にある台風並みの低気圧と季節風とによって生ずるうねりのためで、波高が十㍍に達するものも珍しくない。海の関係者は、西から気圧の谷が近づくので、冬型は一時崩れ、北陸地方の雪もやむが、天気は西日本から下り坂。これを「寒土用波」といって称れる。

〈隆〉

きょうの【天気】

降水確率9〜21時
（21日18時発表）

京都	10%
札幌	60%
仙台	10%
新静	20%
名古屋	40%
大広	30%
福岡	60%
鹿児	80%
那	90%
	70%
	20%

東京　北後南の風晴後

札幌　最時雪
仙台　晴後所どき雪
新潟　晴後一時雨
静岡　晴後時々雨
名古屋　晴・後曇
大阪　曇・後一時雨
広島　晴時々雨
福岡　最後一時雨
鹿児島　最時雨
那覇　晴後曇で一時雨

○快晴　①晴　◎曇　●雨　⊗雪　F霧　風向風力

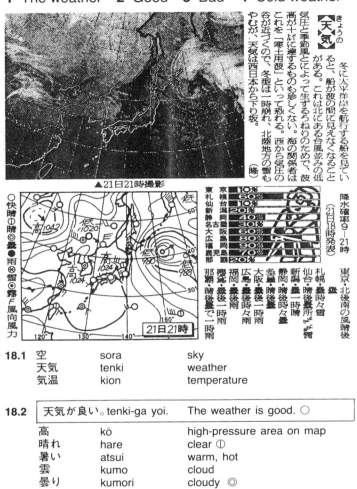

21日21時

18.1	空	sora	sky
	天気	tenki	weather
	気温	kion	temperature

18.2

天気が良い。tenki-ga yoi.	The weather is good. ○

	高	kō	high-pressure area on map
	晴れ	hare	clear ①
	暑い	atsui	warm, hot
	雲	kumo	cloud
	曇り	kumori	cloudy ◎

18.3

天気が悪い。tenki-ga warui.	The weather is bad. ●

18 The Weather

低	tei	low-pressure area on map
雨	ame	rain ●
大雨	ōame	heavy rain
小雨	kosame	light rain
風	fū–, kaze	wind
風雨	fūu	wind and rain
台風	taifū	typhoon
嵐	arashi	storm
傘	kasa	umbrella

18.4

霧	kiri	fog, mist ◉
寒い	samui	cold
霜	shimo	frost
雪	yuki	snow ⊗

Look at this weather map:

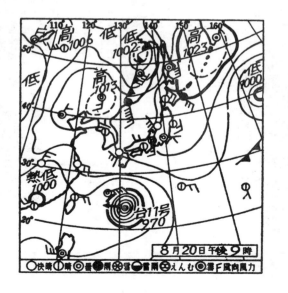

1. What was the weather like in Tokyo?

   . . . .

2. What was the weather like in the extreme south of Japan?

   . . . .

3. What type of wind do you encounter south of Japan?

   . . . .

4. Does this wind move towards Japan?
   Answer 'hai' (yes) or 'iie' (no):

   . . . .

What is the weather like?

5. . . . .   6. . . . .

18 The Weather

7. What is the man holding in his hand to protect himself from the rain? . . . .

8. It's raining and stormy. Say it in Japanese:

. . . .

- The **average temperatures** in Tokyo are 4° centigrade in the winter, 13° in the spring, 25° in the summer and 16.5° in the autumn. In July and August it is very hot and humid.
- In June and in September there is a lot of **rain**.
- In September and October the southern islands of Japan are hard hit by devastating **typhoons**.

---

1 Post office **2** Telephone

9.1	郵便局	yūbin-kyoku	post office, mail
	手紙	tegami	letter (= hand-written)
	切手	kitte	stamp (= strip-off-hand)
	宛名	atena	name and address
	葉書き	hágaki	postcard (= sheet-write)
	絵葉書き	ehágaki	picture postcard
	ポスト	posuto	letter box

19 Post Office, Telephone

絵葉書きがありますか。 ehágaki-ga arimasu ka?	Do you have any picture post-cards? (= Picture-postcards-*subject* there-are *interrogative*.)
このはがきにはる切手 をください。 kono hagaki-ni haru kitte o-kudasái.	I'd like stamps for these post-cards, please. (= These postcards-*indirect-object* stamps-*subject* please.)

19.2	電話	denwa	telephone (= electricity-conversation)
	電話番号	denwa-bangō	telephone number
	電話帳	denwa-chō	telephone directory

もしもし moshi – moshi ピーターです。 Pītā desu.	Hello! Hello! This is Peter speaking. (= Peter to-be.)

What are these called in Japanese?

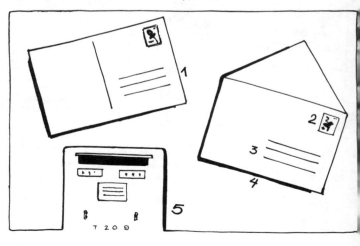

84

1. . . . .   2. . . . .

3. . . . .   4. . . . .

5. . . . .

6. If you can't find any picture postcards in the store, you ask the salesperson:

   . . . .

7. You want to buy stamps for your postcards. You say to the post-office clerk:

   . . . .

```
真 鶴 町 （真鶴　0465）

青木喜義…真、真鶴1162 ……… 真鶴68-2333
青木淳…真、真鶴314 ………… 真鶴68-2722
青木武彦…真、真鶴1162 ……… 真鶴68-1611
                              真鶴68-2333
青木義治…真、真鶴1947 ※(代)真鶴68-2181
味の浜勇…真、真鶴1032 ……… 真鶴68-1232
網元料理入船
       真、真鶴1940 … ※(代)真鶴68-2181
活魚料理いずみ
       真、真鶴1027 ………… 真鶴68-0668
                              真鶴68-2168
磯料理天ぷらうだ川
       真、岩944 …………… 真鶴68-3954
```

8. Which book are these numbers taken from?

   . . . .

9. What are these numbers called?

   . . . .

19 Post Office, Telephone

- A **3-minute local call** costs only 10 yen.
- There are 4 kinds of **public telephones**, each differing in colour and size:

Red telephones:	local and long-distance calls	up to 6 10-yen coins
Blue telephones in public phone booths:	local and long-distance calls	up to 6 10-yen coins
Yellow telephones:	local and international calls	up to 9 100-yen coins
Green telephones:	local, long-distance and international calls	Telephone card & 10 and 100-yen coins

- If you want to **telephone abroad**, ask the operator of your hotel. The charge for a 3-minute call abroad is
  Great Britain, France, West Germany,
    Switzerland, Austria: ¥2,490
  USA, Canada, Mexico, Australia: ¥2,160
- **Postcards** are usually available only in packages, not individually.

航空郵便
Air Mail

標 準 判 Standard Size	第 1 地帯 1st zone	第 2 地帯 2nd zone	第 3 地帯 3rd zone
絵はがきの大きさ Within 107mm × 150mm	¥ 90	¥ 100	¥ 110
	Asia, Australia, New Zealand, Midway & Oceania, etc.	U.S.A., Canada, Central America, West Indies, etc.	All other Countries except 1st 2nd zone. Namely, Middle/Near East, Europe, USSR, Africa, South America and Greenland, etc.

1 Police   **2** Help
3 Doctor   **4** Chemist

20.1	警察	keisatsu	police
	お巡りさん	o-mawari-san	policeman (= Mister 'Going-around')
	交番	kōban	police station

交番はどこですか。 koban-wa doko desu ka?	Where is the nearest police station? (= Police-station-*subject* where be *interrogative*.)
警察を呼んで下さい。 keisatsu-o yonde kudasái.	Call the police, please. (= Police-*direct-object* call please.)
…をなくしました。 ...-o nakushimashita.	I've lost... (...-*direct-object* have-lost.)
私の…が盗まれました。 watashi no ... ga nusumaremashita.	My...has been stolen. (= I-*genitive*...-*subject* is–stolen.)
通訳がほしいです。 tsūyaku ga hoshiidesu	I need an interpreter. (= Interpreter-*subject* desirable.)

20.2	危険	kiken	danger, caution
	助けて	tasuke-te!	Help!
	非常口	hijō-guchi	emergency exit

– The **police** will help you whenever you encounter difficulties, for example if you get lost, if you have lost something, or if you haven't got the correct change for telephoning. There are 1,240 police stations in Tokyo.

---

20 Emergencies

- In case of emergency dial **110** (police).

- It is necessary for you to carry a **valid visa** with you at all times.

- The crime rate is very low; however, look out for **pick-pockets**.

20.3

医	-i-	medicine
医者	isha	doctor (= medicine-personality)
歯医者	haisha	dentist

医者を呼んで下さい。 isha-o yonde kudasái.	Call a doctor, please. (= Doctor-*direct-object* call please.)
私は病気です。 watashi-wa byōki desu.	I'm ill. (= I-*subject* ill be.)
ここが痛い。 kokó-ga itái.	It hurts here. (= Here-*subject* painful.)

20.4

薬	kusuri	medicine (*prescription medication*)
錠剤	jōzai	tablet, pill
ナプキン	napukin	sanitary towel
眼鏡	megane	glasses

- If you fall **ill** in Japan, consult the embassy when selecting a doctor.

- Japanese doctors also sell medicines. **Chemists** are recognised by a green cross.

- **American Pharmacy**   Tel.: 271-4034
  Hibiya Park Bldg., 1 Fl.
  8-1 Yūraku-chō 1-chōme
  Chiyoda-ku, Tokyo 100

English-Japanese Glossary

address 住所 jūsho **2.2**
admission fee 入館料 nyūkan-ryō **16.4**
aeroplane ticket 航空券 kōkū-ken **5.1**
afternoon 午後 go-go **8.2**
airport 空港 kūkō **5.1**
aisle うち uchi **5.3**
aisle-seat 内側 uchigawa **5.3**
American coffee アメリカン amerikan **15.1**
antiques 骨董品 kottōhin **10.1**
appetisers お通し o-tōshi **13.1**
apple りんご ringo **14.2**
apple juice リンゴジュース ringo-jūsu **15.1**
arrival 到着 tōchaku **5.1**
ashtray 灰皿 haizara **15.3**
avenue 道路 dōro **3.2**

bacon ベーコン bēkon **11.4**
bag, briefcase 鞄 kában **2.1**
Baggage claim 荷物引取り nimotsu hikitori **2.1**
bamboo shoots 竹の子 takenoko **14.1**
banana バナナ banana **14.2**
bank 銀行 ginkō **9.2**
battery 電池 denchi **17.3**
be / am / are / is です desu **1.4**
beer ビール bīru **15.2**
big Shinto shrine 神宮 jingū **16.2**
bill 勘定 kanjō **6.3, 9.4**
biscuits クッキー kukkī **14.3**
block 丁目 chōme **4.2**
blouse ブラウス burausu **10.2**
boat, ship 船 fune **5.4**
bonito (fish) かつお katsuo **13.4**
bonsai 盆栽 bonsai **17.2**
bottle 瓶/びん bin **15.2**
bowl for cooked rice, etc. 丼 dómburi **14.1**
bowl of cooked rice and omelet タマゴドン tamago-don **13.3**
brandy ブランデー burándē **15.2**
bread パン pan **11.3**
breakfast 朝食 chōshoku **11.1**
bridge 橋 hashi **3.2**
brochure, pamphlet パンフレット panfuretto **16.1**
Buddha 仏 hotake **16.2**
Buddhist temple 寺 tera **16.2**
Bullet train 新幹線 Shin-kan-sen **5.3**
bus バス basu **5.2**
butter バター batā **11.3**

calling card 名刺 mei-shi **2.2**
camera カメラ kámera **17.3**
car 車 kuruma **3.1**
car rental レンタカー renta-kā **3.1**
carrots にんじん ninjin **14.1**
cash-desk お勘定場 o-kanjōba **9.4**
cashier (reception) フロント会計 furonto-kaikei **6.3**
cassette カセット kasetto **10.3**
castle 城 shiro **16.2**
cherry blossom 桜 sakura **17.2**
chicken drumstick もも mómo **13.3**
chocolate チョコレート chokorēto **14.3**
chop-sticks おはし o-hashi **11.2**
chrysanthemum 菊 kiku **17.2**
cigarette たばこ tábako **15.3**
city map 市内地図 shinai-chizu **4.1**
city centre 市内 shi-nai **4.1**
clear 晴れ hare **18.2**
closing day 本日休業 hónjitsu kyūgyō **9.3**
clothes (Western-style) 洋服 yō-fuku **10.2**
cloud 雲 kumo **18.2**
cloudy 曇り kumori **18.2**
coca cola コカコーラ koka-kōra **15.1**
coffee コーヒー kōhī **11.3, 15.1**
cold 寒い samui **18.4**
computer コンピューター kompyūtā **10.3**
consulate 領事館 ryōji-kan **2.3**
control, check 検査 kensa **2.1**
cooked rice ご飯 gohan **14.1**
cotton コットン kotton **10.2**
cup カップ kappu **11.2**
customs 税関 zeikan **2.1**

danger 危険 kiken **20.2**
day, sun 日 hi **8.2**
dentist 歯医者 haisha **20.3**
department store デパート depáto **9.3**
departure 出発 shuppatsu **5.1**
dessert デザート dezáto **14.3**
dining hall 食堂 shokudō **12.1**
dinner, supper 夕食 yúshoku **11.1**
direct object を -o
discount price 割引 waribiki **9.4**
doctor 医者 isha **20.3**
doll 人形 ningyō **10.1**
dollar ドル doru **9.1**
domestic air lines 国内線 kokunai-sen **5.1**

English-Japanese Glossary

drawing 図 zu **4.1**
drive 運転する unten-suru **3.1**
driver 運転手 unten-shu **3.1**
driving licence 運転免許証 unten-menkyoshō **3.1**

earthquake 地震 jishin **17.1**
east 東 higashi **4.2**
eat, appetite 食 shoku **11.1**
eel うなぎ unagi **13.4**
egg タマゴ tamago **11.3, 13.3**
electric train 電車 densha **5.3**
electronic equipment 電子器具 denshi-kigu **10.3**
embassy 大使館 taishí-kan **2.3**
emergency exit 非常口 hijōguchi **6.2, 20.2**
emperor 皇 kō **16.2**
emperor's palace 皇居 kōkyo **16.2**
entrance 入口 iriguchi **16.4**
evening, night 夜 yoru **8.2**
exchange 両替 ryōgae **9.2**
excuse me すみません sumimasen **1.1**
exit 出口 deguchi **3.2, 16.4**
expensive 高い taka-i **1.3, 9.4**

fan うちわ uchiwa **10.1**
February 2月 nigatsu **8.3**
ferry フェリー ferī **5.4**
film フィルム firumu **17.3**
first-class carriage グリーン車 grīn-sha **5.3**
first name 人名 jin-mei **2.2**
fish 魚 sakana **13.4**
fish broth 出し／だし dashi **12.3**
flash フラッシュ furasshu **17.3**
flavoured shaved ice 氷 kōri **14.3**
flight 便 bin **5.1**
flight number 便名 bin-mei **5.1**
flower 花 hana **17.2**
flower arranging 生け花 ikebana **17.2**
fog, mist 霧 kiri **18.4**
for hire, free 空車 kūsha **3.4**
foreigners 外人 gai-jin **2.2**
fork フォーク fōku **11.2**
Friday 金曜日 kin-yōbi **8.3**
frost 霜 shimo **18.4**

garden 園 -en **17.2**
gate (airport) ゲート gēto **5.1**
gate (temple) 鳥居 torii **16.2**
genitive の -no
Gentlemen 男性 dansei **6.4**

ginger 生姜 shōga **12.3**
glass グラス gurasu **11.2**
glasses 眼鏡 megane **20.4**
goodbye さようなら sayōnara **1.1**
good morning おはようございます ohayō gozaimasu **1.1**
great Buddha 大仏 daibutsu **16.2**
green tea お茶 o-cha **15.1**
ground floor 1階／1F ikkai **6.2**
group 団体 dantai **16.1**
guide ガイド gaido **16.1**

hand luggage 手荷物 tenimotsu **2.1**
ham ハム hamu **11.4**
heavy rain 大雨 ōame **18.3**
hello こんにちは konnichi-wa **1.1**
hello! hello! (telephone) もしもし moshi – moshi **19.2**
help! 助けて tasuke-te! **20.2**
high-pressure area 高 kō **18.2**
hotel ホテル hoteru **6.1**

ice-cream アイスクリーム aisukurīmu **14.3**
indirect object に -ni
information 案内所 annaijo **5.3**
international lines 国際線 kokusai-sen **5.1**
interrogative か ka
island 島 shima **17.1**

Japanese drama 能 nō **16.3**

key 鍵／カギ kagi **6.2**
kimono 着物 ki-mono **10.2**
kiosk, stand 売店 baiten **9.3**
knife ナイフ naifu **11.2**

lacquer ware 漆器 shikki **10.1**
Ladies 女性 josei **6.4**
late in the afternoon 夕方 yū-gata **8.2**
left 左 hidári **4.2**
lemon レモン remon **14.3**
lens レンズ renzu **17.3**
letter 手紙 tégami **19.1**
letter box ポスト posuto **19.1**
lift エレベーター erebētā **6.2**
light rain 小雨 kosame **18.3**
line 線 sen **5.3**
liver レバー rebā **13.2**
low-pressure area on map 低 tei **18.3**
luggage 荷物 nimotsu **2.1**
lunch 昼食 chūshoku **11.1**

English-Japanese Glossary

map 地図 chizu **4.1**
March 3月… san gatsu **8.3**
matches マッチ matchi **15.3**
meal 食事 shokuji **11.1**
meal coupon 食券 shokken **12.2**
meat 肉 niku **13.2**
menu メニュー ményū **12.2**
medicine (science) 医 -i- **20.3**
medicine 薬 kursuri **20.4**
melon メロン meron **14.3**
microcomputer マイコン maikon **10.3**
milk ミルク miruku **11.3**
minute 分 fun **8.1**
Monday 月曜日 gétsu-yobi **8.3**
money お金 o-kane **9.1**
month 月 gatsu, tsuki **8.3**
morning 朝 asa **8.2**
motorway 高速道路 kōsoku-dōro **3.2**
mountain 山 -san, yama **17.1**
Mount Fuji 富士山 fujisan **17.1**
municipal district 区 ku **4.1**
museum 博物館 hakubútsu-kan **16.2**

name お名前 o-namae **2.2**
name and address 宛名 atena **19.1**
nation 国 kuni **2.3**
nationality 国籍 kokuseki **2.3**
national railways 国鉄 koku-tetsu **5.3**
national suburban train 国電 koku-den **5.3**
no いいえ iie **1.1**
non-residents 非居住者 hi kyojūsha **2.1**
noodles (buckwheat) そば soba **13.1**
noodles (white) うどん udon **13.1**
north 北 kita **4.2**
no smoking 禁煙 kin-en **15.3**
no smoking carriage 禁煙車 kin-en-sha **5.3**

oden (fish cakes) おでん oden **13.4**
oil オイル oiru **3.3**
onion 玉ねぎ tamanegi **14.1**
orange オレンジ orenji **14.2**
orange juice オレンジジュース orenji-jūsu **15.1**

painful 痛い ita-i
park 公園 kōen **17.2**
passport 旅券 ryoken **2.2**
passport パスポート pasupōto **2.2**
passport control 旅券検査 ryoken kensa **2.1**

paying 支払い shiharái **12.4**
pearls 真珠 shinjú **10.1**
pepper コショウ koshō **12.3**
personal computer パソコン pasokon **10.3**
petrol ガソリン gasorin **3.3**
petrol station ガソリンスタンド gasorin-sutando **3.3**
photo 写真 sha-shin **17.3**
photo shop カメラ店 kamera-ten **17.3**
picture postcard 絵葉書き ehágaki **19.1**
piece (books) つ -satsu **7.2**
piece (bottles etc.) 枚 -bon / hon **7.2**
piece (machines) 台 -dai **7.2**
piece (objects) 冊 -tsu **7.2**
piece (thin articles) 本 -mai **7.2**
pine tree 松 matsu **17.2**
plate, dish 皿 sara **11.2**
platform のりば noríba **5.3**
plum wine 梅酒 ume-shu **15.2**
plural たち -tachi
pocket calculator ポケット計算器 poketto keisanki **10.3**
police 警察 keisatsu **20.1**
policeman お巡りさん o-mawari-san **20.1**
police station 交番 kōban **20.1**
polite prefix お o-
polite prefix ご go-
pork chop とんかつ tonkatsu **13.2**
port 港 minato **5.4**
postcard 葉書き hágaki **19.1**
post office, mail 郵便局 yūbin-kyoku **19.1**
pottery 陶器 tōki **10.1**
price 値段/ねだん nedan **9.4**
private railway 私鉄 shi-tetsu **5.3**
pull 引く hiku **16.4**
pullover, sweater セーター sétā **10.2**
push 押す osu **16.4**

radio ラジオ rajio **10.3**
radish 大根 daikon **14.1**
railway 鉄道 tetsu-do **5.3**
rain 雨 ame **18.3**
raw fish 寿司/鮨/すし sushi **11.4**
raw rice 米 komé **14.1**
razor 電気カミソリ denki kamisori **6.4**
reception desk フロント furonto **6.2**
record レコード rekōdo **10.3**
reservation 予約 yoyaku **5.3, 6.2**
residents 居住者 kyojūsha **2.1**

English-Japanese Glossary

restaurant レストラン résutoran **12.1**
rice wine 酒 sake **15.2**
right 右 migi **4.2**
river 川 kawa **17.1**
road 国道 kokudō **3.2**
road map 道路地図 dōro-chizu **4.1**
room 部屋 heya **6.2**

salt 塩 shio **12.3**
sandwich サンドウィッきま sandoittchi **11.4**
sanitary towel ナプキン napukin **20.4**
Saturday 土曜日 do-yōbi **8.3**
sea, ocean 海 umi **17.1**
seaweed (for broth) のり kombu **14.1**
seaweed (for rice)こんぶnori **14.1**
seaweed (in soup) わかめ wakame **14.1**
second 秒 byō **8.1**
second floor 2階 nikai **6.2**
self-service セルフサービス serufu sābisu **9.3**
Shinto 神道 shintō **16.2**
Shinto shrine 神社 jinja **16.2**
shirt シャツ shatsu **10.2**
shoes 靴 kutsu **10.2**
shop, store 店 mise **9.3**
shrimp, prawn えび ebi **13.4**
silk 絹 kinu **10.2**
sky 天 ten **18.1**
sliced raw fish 刺身 sáshimi **13.4**
slide スライド suraído **17.3**
snack 軽食 keishoku **11.4**
snow 雪 yuki **18.4**
soap 石けん sekken **6.4**
software ソフトウエア sofutouea **10.3**
soup, broth スープ sūpu **13.1**
south 南 minami **4.2**
soy bean 大豆 daizu **14.1**
soybean curd 豆腐 tōfu **14.1**
soya bean paste みそ miso **14.1**
soy sauce 醤油 shōyu **12.3**
spoon スプーン supūn **11.2**
stamp 切手 kitte **19.1**
station 駅 eki **5.3**
statue of the Buddha 仏像 butsuzō **16.2**
stereo set ステレオ sutereo **10.3**
storm 嵐 arashi **18.3**
straight ahead まっすぐ massúgu **4.2**
strawberry イチゴ ichigo **14.3**
... street ...通り dōri **3.2**
subject は -wa **1.3**
subject が -ga **1.3**

subway 地下鉄 chiká-tetsu **5.2**
sugar 砂糖 satō **12.3**
sukiyaki すき焼き sukiyaki **13.2**
Sunday 日曜日 nichi-yōbi **8.3**
supermarket スーパー sūpā **9.3**
sweet rice wine みりん mirin **12.3**

table テーブル tēburu **12.2**
tablet, pill 錠剤 jōzai **20.4**
tap water 水 mizu **15.1**
'tatami' mat 畳 tatami **12.2**
tax-free shop 免税店 menzeiten **9.4**
taxi タクシー takushī **3.4, 5.2**
tea (green) お茶 o-cha **11.3**
tea (black) 紅茶 kōcha **15.1**
tea shop, café 喫茶店 kissaten **12.1**
telephone 電話 denwa **19.2**
telephone directory 電話帳 denwa-chō **19.2**
telephone number 電話番号 denwa-bangō **19.2**
telephoto lens 望遠レンズ bōen-renzu **17.3**
temperature 気温 kion **18.1**
tempura 天ぷら tempura **13.4**
Tenno 天皇 tennō **16.2**
thank you ありがとう arigatō **1.1**
thank you very much どうもありがとう dōmo arigatō **1.1**
traditional play 歌舞伎 kabuki **16.3**
there あそこ asóko **4.2**
there is / are あります ari-masu **1.4**
there is / are not ありません ari-masen **1.4**
Thursday 木曜日 moku-yōbi **8.3**
ticket 切符 kippu **5.3**
time, hour 時間 jikan **8.1**
toast トースト tōsuto **11.3**
today 今日 kyō **8.2**
toilets トイレ tóire **6.4**
toll gate 料金所 ryōkinjo **3.2**
tomorrow 明日 ashita **8.2**
tourism, sightseeing 観光 kankō **16.1**
tourist 観光客 kankō-kyaku **16.1**
town 市 shi **4.1**
transfer, change のりかえ norikae **5.2**
transistor トランジスター toranjisutā **10.3**
Tuesday 火曜日 ka-yōbi **8.3**
tuna まぐろ maguro **13.4**
typhoon 台風 taifū **18.3**

English-Japanese Glossary

umbrella 傘 kasa **18.3**

vanilla バニラ banira **14.3**
vegetables 野菜 yasai **14.1**
vinegar 酢 su **12.3**
volcano 火山 kazan **17.1**

waiter ウエイター ueitā **12.4**
warm, hot 暑い atsui **18.2**
watch 時計 tokéi **8.1**
watch 腕時計 ude-dokei **10.3**
weather 天気 tenki **18.1**
Wednesday 水曜日 sui-yōbi **8.3**
week 週 shū **8.3**
west 西 nishi **4.2**

when いつ itsu **8.1**
where どこ doko **4.2**
wind 風 fū, kaze **18.3**
wind and rain 風雨 fūu **18.3**
window まど mado **5.3**
window 窓側 madogawa **5.3**
whisky ウイスキー uisukī **15.2**
wool ウール ūru **10.2**
wrestling 相撲 sumō **16.3**

yakitori やきとり yakitori **13.3**
year 年 toshi **8.3**
yen 円(￥)en **9.1**
yes, well, O.K. はい hai **1.1**
yesterday 昨日 kinō **8.2**
yoghurt ヨーグルト yōguruto **11.3**

Answers

p 13 1. ohayō gozaimasu 2. konnichi-wa 3. Igirisu-jin desu ka? 4. hai 5. iie 6. (dōmo) arigatō 7. sayōnara 8. sumimasen

pp 16–17 1. queue at the 'hi kyojūsha' （非居住者） 2. nimotsu hikitori （荷物引取り） 3. 税関 (zeikan) 4. nimotsu 5. meishi 6. Eikoku taishi-kan 7. Jap. nihon Eng. Japan 8. Jap. nihon-jin Eng. Japanese 9. Jap. gai-jin Eng. aliens 10. foreign country (outside-country)

pp 20–21 1. kuruma 2. gasorin-sutando 3. mantan-ni shite kudasai 4. takushī 5. 空車 kūsha 6. Nippon-hoteru e itte kudasai 7. ikura desu ka? 8. deguchi 9. ryōkinjo 10. chūsha kinshi

pp 24–25 1. shinai-chizu-o ichimai kudasai 2. eki-wa doko desu ka? 3. nishi-deguchi wa doko desu ka? 4. massugu desu 5. (dōmo) arigatō 6. hidari-e 7. migi-e 8. hidari-e / massugu

pp 28–29 1. kūkō-e itte kudasai 2. 出発 shuppatsu 3. 国内線 kokunai-sen 4. 国際線 kokusai-sen 5. tsugi-no eki wa doko desu ka? 6. shinjuku-yuki-wa dore desu ka? 7. hiroshima-yuki-no kippu-o ichimai kudasai 8. grin-sha 9. madogawa-no seki-o kudasai (seki = seat) 10. kippu 11. ferī or fune

pp 33–34 1. beddo 2. kagi 3. futari-yō-no heya-o kudasai 4. nihaku 5. yoyaku shimashita 6. erebētā wa doko desuka? 7. hijōguchi 8. denki kamisori 9. sekken 10. toire-wa doko desuka?

pp 37–38 1. hyaku-go (gō shitsu) (add 'gō shitsu' to express a room number) 2. sen-hyaku (gō shitsu) 3. go-hyaku ni-jū (gō shitsu) 4. ni-hyaku san-jū (gō shitsu) 5. hyaku-ni-jū-yon 6. jū shichi (nichi) (add 'nich' to a date) 7. jū kyū K 8. hyaku-ni-jū en 9. go-jū en

pp 40–41 1. fun (but one minute = 'ippun') 2. jikan 3. nichi 4. shūkan (but one week = 'isshūkan' 5. nen 6. tokei 7. go ji 8. hachi ji 9. jū ji 10. jū ji han 11. Jap. hi Engl. day / sun 12. Jap. gatsu / tsuki Engl. month / moon

pp 45–46 1. 銀行 ginkō 2. ryōgae-wa doko de dekimasuka? 3. hyaku pondo-o ryōgae shite kudasai 4. ikura desuka? 5. kaite kudasai 6. waribiki 7. san-byaku en 8. sen-nana-hyaku go-jū en

pp 49–50 1. kimono 2. shinju 3. shikki 4. sutereo 5. kamera 6. poketto keisanki 7. kore-o misete kudasai 8. kore-o morai masu / kore-o kudasai

pp 52–54 1. chō shoku 2. chūshoku 3. yūshoku 4. kappu 5. gurasu 6. (o)-hashi 7. fōku 8. sara 9. naifu 10. spūn 11. fōku o kudasai 12. sushi or o-sushi

p 57 1. kissaten 2. shokudō 3. resutoran 4. kore-o kudasai 5. kore-wa ikura desu ka? 6. shio 7. koshō 8. shōyu 9. o-kanjō-o shitai / o-kanjō-o onegaishimasu

pp 60–62 1. soba or udon 2. maguro 3. katsuo 4. unagi 5. ebi 6. yakitori 7. tamago-don 8. roppyaku en

pp 64–66 1. tamanegi 2. ninjin 3. daikon 4. ringo 5. orenji 6. banana 7. kōri 8. kōri-ichigo 9. kōri-meron 10. banira-aisukurīmu

pp 69–70 1. (koka-) kōra-o hitotsu kudasai 2. bīru-o ippon kudasai 3. orenji-jūsu-o hitotsu kudasai 4. sei-shu 5. (o-)mizu o kudasai 6. o-cha o kudasai 7. たばこ tabako

pp 73–74 1. nagoya-jō 2. kinkaku-ji 3. daibutsu 4. torii 5. deguchi (exit) 6. kabuki 7. sumō

pp 76–78 1. Jap. yama Engl. mountain 2. Jap. kawa Engl. river 3. fuji-san 4. matsu 5. bonsai 6. kamera 7. bōen renzu 8. renzu 9. firumu 10. furasshu

pp 81–82 1. kumori (cloudy) 2. hare (clear) 3. taifū (typhoon) 4. iie 5. fūu 6. hare / atsui 7. kasa (umbrella) 8. arashi / taifū

pp 85–86 1. ehagaki 2. kitte 3. atena 4. tegami 5. posuto 6. ehagaki-ga arimasu ka? 7. kono hagaki-ni kitte o kudasai 8. denwa-chō 9. denwa-bangō